I'M WRONG.

I'M SORRY.

I LOVE YOU.

Getting along with your mate after a squabble.

A survival manual for men.

by

Dr. Art Shulman

Copyright © 2016 by Art Shulman

All rights reserved. No part of this publication may be reproduced, stored in a retrieval system, or transmitted, in any form or by any means, electronic, mechanical, photocopying, recording, or otherwise, without the prior written permission of the copyright owner.

Printed in the United States of America
ISBN 978-0-9983809-6-4

This manual is…
dedicated to women everywhere.

(But I hope they don't read it)

WHY READ THIS BOOK?

Here's what this manual is about.

Or not about. This book is not intended to demean or diminish women. Just the opposite.

Women today are not the meek subservient 'gentler sex' portrayed in the distant past. You will never catch me calling Rebecca, my wife, 'The little woman,' or 'The little lady,' or 'My better half.' Even less likely is me calling her, 'My old lady' (*though I might do it years and years from now when she is really old in years and proud of it*).

Today's women are smart. (*Rebecca, of course, says they always were.*) Well, not all of them are smart. But yours is, isn't she? After all, you're not so stupid as to marry or go steady with a nitwit, are you? Even one of average intelligence. Of course she's not as smart as you. But still smart.

To illustrate how women have become more independent, and how gender behavior has changed, even flip-flopped, in recent years (*and this may be due to where I reside -- Los Angeles*), when I go to a party I seem to notice that the women are more likely than men to drink alcohol. (*Didn't it used to be the opposite?*)

When I asked Rebecca why it might be the case that women are more likely than men to drink alcohol, she didn't deny it. She just said, "It may have something to do with the men they came to the party with." (*Of course she wasn't talking about herself.*)

See, women are asserting themselves these days.

At any rate, you, the man of the house, have established a relationship with her and she for sure has qualities which have attracted you and continue to attract you. (*Of course, over time, you no doubt have noticed that she – not Rebecca, of course -- has a few qualities that have gradually become annoying. But you have annoying qualities too. Maybe fewer than she has, but some.*)

You have an intimate relationship with her, likely love her, even if it's just for the most part. (*But, of course, the whole part for me with Rebecca*). And like all relationships it must be managed, attention paid, cared for benevolently, and as with plants, needs to be fed and watered periodically, especially if, when she gets all dolled up, she looks like an exquisite flower.

But I'm not suggesting you add plant food to her herbal tea, or pour water over her head. (*Hint: If you're going to water her head do it by sprinkling from a watering can, not dousing it sloppily with a few gallons' worth of hose water, which is the type of thing she might do to you if she's angry enough.*)

Just treat her well and she will blossom. (*Of course, if she's really angry at you she may tell you in no uncertain terms, "I don't exactly need you to help me blossom."*)

As with most relationships you two don't *always* get along. So to continue your (*hopefully*) wonderful relationship, to diminish household tension, to enhance your peace of mind, you need to handle the instances of negative interaction which, if left to fester, may turn awfully unnerving and disagreeable. You must become a manager of sorts. Not a victim of dispute.

This manual is designed to help you do that -- handle the aftermath of those unpleasant interactions which can happen with any relationship. (*Notice I use words such as 'manage' and 'handle' here. I don't use the word 'control', as that would suggest you are a 'controlling' person, a negative label you don't want to be associated with. Even if you are.*)

And to help with this managing and handling, I suggest approaching her with a very simple message after you have these negative exchanges:

I'm wrong.
I'm sorry.
I love you.

SHOULD YOU LET YOUR MATE KNOW YOU BOUGHT THIS BOOK?

The answer is…

NO!!!

Let me state that again.

NO!!!

If you coached a football team would you want the other team to have your playbook ahead of the important upcoming game? (*Yes, relationships are a game of sorts.*)

The other side could anticipate your plays, scheme to stop them so you gain no yardage. Or even worse, make you lose yardage. Make you fumble. Intercept your passes. And they'll be able to score on you. (*No, not that type of score.*)

If she knows you own this book she won't go out and purchase her own copy. She'll just ask to read yours. Where does that lead?

Not only will she know your game plan, but if she reads your copy it means fewer copies of this book are sold. Fewer sales means less money for me. But I'm willing to forego that, perhaps because I'm by nature altruistic, trying to make the world a better, less tense place to live.

Accumulating money for the sake of money is not my main motivation. But it is an important secondary motivation. I do like lobster and bouillabaisse. But more important, having lots of money, in addition to providing for a comfortable retirement, will allow me the sustenance to write additional books valuable to mankind. (*Is there a 'womankind'?*)

Future books I'm thinking of include:

HOW TO ELIMINATE WORLD HUNGER – THE POTENTIAL OF AMOEBA FARMS

THE RENEWABLE ENERGY SOURCE THAT EVERY MAN HAS INSIDE HIS JOCK

THE THRILLING EARLY HISTORY OF THE AMERICAN ACCOUNTING ASSOCIATION

7 STEPS TO BECOMING A GRANDMASTER AT TIC TAC TOE

THE BEST STRATEGIES TO GET OUT OF JAIL IN THE GAME OF MONOPOLY

HOW TO PRACTICE IMPROV COMEDY AT A FUNERAL

HOW TO SAFELY DRIVE A CAR IN REVERSE ON THE FREEWAY

HOW TO PICK UP GIRLS IN THE HOSPITAL EMERGENCY ROOM

50 PROVEN WAYS TO CLEAN A SOMBRERO

HOW TO COMMIT SUICIDE WITHOUT KILLING YOURSELF

BEST METHODS FOR WASHING SOCKS AFTER PLAYING BASKETBALL

1001 WAYS TO USE A TABLESPOON

Also, a best-selling book means fame, admiration *(or is it jealousy)* from my peers, and self-satisfaction in proving my kindergarten teacher wrong when she said I'd never amount to anything. (*She was ultimately fired when the principal made a surprise visit in the midst of her calling out to the whole class of six year-olds, "You're all a bunch of losers".*)

And a best-seller on this subject gratifies me by knowing I'm helping others keep their healthy personal relationship with a mate.

But the major driving force underlying this literary effort is to improve the lot of us guys.

At any rate, **do NOT let your mate know you have this book!**

Do not bring it out in her presence.

Do not leave it in a place where she would notice it.

And do not bring up the book's existence in conversations with her or her blabbermouth friends and family. (*If she's a woman she undoubtedly has at least several blabbermouth friends.*)

Just use the information it imparts.

And if for some reason she initiates discussion of the book, perhaps because she has deviously already purchased it, play dumb that you already have your own copy.

Also, if she somehow already has a copy, beware; do not use the contents of this book in an obvious manner, as she may notice your strategy and recognize you've been hiding this manual, diminishing her trust in you.

If somehow she does find out you have a copy, merely say you'd been planning it as a gift for her on the next appropriate occasion. And if she questions why there are pages marked with a yellow highlighter, if you were going to gift her, explain that you were just trying to make her life easier by highlighting the important parts.

But if she doesn't believe you, and there is no alternative, just say, "I'm wrong. I'm sorry. I love you."

Happy reading!

WHICH IS THE MOST IMPORTANT CHAPTER IN THIS BOOK?

This one.

The prime objectives of this book are to ensure that couples' lives aren't filled with discord and acrimony, and instead help pairs be happy with each other by repairing rifts between them.

While most of this book discusses behavior *after* a rift occurs, in reality the best way to ensure that you're not in the midst of having to resolve a schism is to *avoid having one in the first place*.

How is that most effectively done?

Any woman will tell you that the best way to treat her, the unsurpassed way to keep peace, *before* you get into a rift of any sort, is to just say, "You're right." (*Alternatively you can use the old standby, 'Yes, dear.'*)

If you want a harmonious life with her, *even if you think she's wrong*, tell her she's right.

For example, if she says your blue tie looks better on you than the red one, say, "You're right."

If she changes her mind and says the red tie looks better on you than the blue, say, "You're right."

If she says Sam Schmidlap is a far better actor than Marlon Brando ever was, say, "You're right."

Get the point? Even if you know she's wrong, say, "You're right."

Even if you know *she knows she's wrong*, to keep peace, say, "You're right."

Whether it's a matter of opinion or of fact, say, "You're right."

Of course, make sure it's a situation where you won't be placed in great jeopardy. Like, if she says, "Don't worry. That white shark lingering offshore isn't interested in biting you, so jump right in that silly ocean," you might not want to say, "You're right." (*Well, maybe you should say, "You're right" because that will keep her happy. Just make sure you don't actually jump into the silly ocean. Also, be very suspicious of her really wanting to preserve your relationship.*)

Or, if she says, "That bully may be fifty pounds heavier than you and knows taekwondo, but you should beat him up because he looked at me funny." (*Again, maybe you should say she's right, but add you can't fight just now because you want to avoid spilling his blood in this nice café.*)

Anyway, the rule is, **<u>BEFORE</u> YOU HAVE THAT RIFT, TO PREVENT IT FROM HAPPENING, TELL YOUR MATE 'YOU'RE RIGHT' AS OFTEN AS NEEDED.**

If you follow this rule you'll enormously lower the likelihood of needing to say, "I'm wrong. I'm sorry. I love you," or even (*to be dealt with later*) "You're right. I'm sorry. I love you."

NOTE: Remember, there is a difference between saying 'You're right' by itself, and as a preface to 'I'm sorry. I love you.'

SPAT, DISAGREEMENT, ARGUMENT, SQUABBLE, TIFF, QUARREL

There are six words I've found which some might think amount to the same thing -- Spat, Squabble, Tiff, Quarrel, Argument, Disagreement.

Turns out they're *not* the same thing. They differ in gravitas. Some are more 'serious' than others.

To help determine the order I did a short survey among 110 people I know, about half men and half women, asking them to rank those six words in order of 'seriousness', with 1 being most serious and 6 being least serious. (*Why 110 people? Is it because that number of cornets were close at hand to 76 trombones in The Music Man? No. It's because of the 125 people I asked to respond, 15 said no because the task seemed stupid to them.*)

These 110 folks are not exactly typical of the general populace. They're more intelligent and educated as a group, but may be a little weird, since they *are* associated with me in some way.

However, I think the results would hold up if I interviewed all the intelligent and educated English speaking adults in the United States. Which I'm not even going to attempt, because most people don't know me and when I approached them would think I'm weird, asking them to do that odd task of ranking six words. After all, how would you feel if a total stranger ambushed you and said, "Pardon me, would you rank six words in order of seriousness?"

I don't know about you, but I find it hard to handle rejection.

Another reason is that it would take me a long time to interview a couple of hundred million people. And I have other books to write in my bucket list.

Wait! I mentioned interviewing just 'intelligent and educated' people. Restricting it to intelligent and educated people (*like you*) might reduce the number of folks to be interviewed by 95%.

But still not practically doable.

This chart shows the percentages given each word, broken into 3 groups – most serious (*ranking of 1 or 2*), medium serious (*ranking of 3 or 4*), and least serious (*ranking of 5 or 6*).

WORD	Most Serious (1 or 2)	Medium Serious (3 or 4)	Least Serious (5 or 6)
Argument	76%	17%	7%
Quarrel	51%	23%	6%
Disagreement	31%	34%	35%
Squabble	21%	44%	35%
Spat	18%	39%	43%
Tiff	4%	31%	70%

The consensus deemed 'argument' the most serious, followed by 'quarrel'.

'Tiff' was deemed the least serious.

Here's a simplified presentation of the consensus order, a continuum of sorts, with the most serious listed first:

Argument
Quarrel
Disagreement
Squabble
Spat
Tiff

One noteworthy finding is that 'disagreement' is ranked about equally as most serious (31%), medium serious (34%), and least serious (35%). So, when a person talks about having a disagreement, we can't offer a good guess on how serious it was. All the other five terms tend in one direction. (*Isn't that interesting! There's major disagreement about the word 'disagreement.'*)

What is special about 'disagreement'? As one lady I interviewed pointed out, "Two people can legitimately disagree on some issue without it resulting in tension between them." (*In other words, it doesn't have to become an argument, or even a quarrel, or even a tiff. Just an intellectual thing that can even be fun to debate.*)

So, since we can't really be sure what 'disagreement' connotes, I promise not to use that term in this manual any further. And if I somehow do accidentally use the word 'disagreement' (*Oops! I just broke my promise!*), you have the right to never buy this manual again.

At any rate, your wife is much more likely to bash you over the head, threaten to divorce you, give you the silent treatment, withhold mattress privileges, and burn all your underwear if you have an 'argument' than if you have a 'tiff'.

This manual deals with malfeasances ranging from tiffs to squabbles, and not with the more serious 'quarrel' or 'argument' malfeasances. (*Examples of the latter two major no-noes are having an outside romantic affair, or gambling away your retirement savings in Vegas shooting craps.*)

For these types of dastardly behaviors you'll need a lot more than this book. Perhaps a marriage counselor (*not biased against men*). Or, more likely, a divorce attorney.

Of course, your wife may consider what you think is minor as major. And she's always right. If she considers it major, then it is. As one example, once I took bagels that had been toasted out of the toaster and inserted my own bagel. When my beautiful wife Rebecca noticed her bagel on the countertop she verbally assaulted me about taking her bagel out and not informing her. When I tried to diminish my malfeasance (*which I didn't even think was wrong*), she hammered me verbally about this being another example of my not caring.

I don't recall how that situation was resolved (*I probably just said, "You're right"* – *not about not caring, but about removing the bagel*), though it ultimately was. After all, we're still married (*unless she got a divorce I don't know about*).

Also, what seems minor may quickly degenerate into something major. That's why it's important to deal with tiffs, spats and squabbles before they evolve into quarrels and arguments.

This middle ground of 'squabble' is why the subtitle of this book is, "How to get along with your mate after a *squabble*." 'Squabble' is in the middle of the continuum.

By the way, Rebecca doesn't think I have the correct order. She thinks a 'squabble' is less serious than 'spat'. We've had a tiff about that. No, it was not resolved by my saying, "I'm wrong. I'm sorry. I love you."

There are some things you just don't give in on.

DON'T FORGET THE 'I LOVE YOU'

EVEN THOUGH THIS IS ONE OF THE SHORTEST CHAPTERS IN THIS MANUAL, IT MAY BE THE SECOND MOST IMPORTANT CHAPTER, AFTER THE ONE ON NOT GETTING INTO RIFTS IN THE FIRST PLACE!

DON'T FORGET THE 'I LOVE YOU!'

This 'love' message really gets through to women. All will be forgiven if you love her and tell her so.

Well, not necessarily *all*.

But some things, especially small stuff – the stuff that causes tiffs, spats, and squabbles.

Saying you love her in those instances will get you far!

But, in the event of a rift, not as far as prefacing it with, "I'm wrong. I'm sorry."

Some, like my wife Rebecca, will even say you should *frequently* tell her you love her, since if you do, you may not ever need to avoid having a rift. That is, once you say you love her, she won't let a situation progress into a rift.

(By the way, don't tell your mate you love her frequently, because then – especially if she's picky -- she'll ask you, "You love me frequently? When don't you love me?"

Your best answer is "Never," but that might not get you off.

Instead, as I said, frequently tell her that you love her. Word order is important.

I wonder what's going to happen when Rebecca notices I'm using her name in this book. I suppose if she complains I'll just say, "I'm wrong. I'm sorry. I love you."

But that might not work. She's on to me. She'll say something like, "I've heard that before."

So, I'll continue, "You're wonderful and I want to brag on you and show you off to the world."

"Really?" she might ask.

"Truly," I'll respond.

And then she'll give me that meaningful wink.

Sure. Well, a man can dream, can't he?

WHERE DID 'I'M WRONG. I'M SORRY. I LOVE YOU' COME FROM?

I first heard the speech, "I'm wrong. I'm sorry. I love you" from a friend, who was commenting on what one should do when wanting to resolve a rift with another close person.

My friend said he didn't make up the phrase, but heard it from his therapist. The therapist was apologizing to him for losing his temper and telling my friend during a session, "Why can't you just get your act together!" (*This worried my friend no end – his therapist telling him he loved him – reverse transference. So he stopped seeing that one, and is seeing another psychotherapist. They are now at the point, when delving into my friend's early childhood, of working through his mother saying to him, "Why can't you just get your act together!"*)

I googled the statement, and the closest reference was a song released in 2013 by a folk country & Western singer named Derek Webb with his song, "I Was Wrong, I'm Sorry, & I Love You."

But I'm not sure Derek was the originator. He might have been. Or, it could have been said previously and Derek picked it up. Even if Derek says he originated it, he might've unconsciously registered something he'd heard previously. Derek won't intentionally lie. He's religious. Religious people don't *usually* promulgate big lies. Unless it's a priest or Cardinal talking about boys.

Who knows? Maybe the phrase comes from antiquity, olden times. Because men and women didn't always get along, did they?

Like King Louis XVI of France saying, "I'm wrong. I'm sorry. I love you" to his wife, Queen Marie Antoinette, after she exclaimed, "What? You ate the whole rest of my cake just because you were hungry!"

Or, even before that, when the wife of Socrates said, "I'm wrong. I'm sorry. I love you," after her husband exclaimed, "What? You threw out my hemlock antidote that I planned to hide in my toga?"

At any rate, the saying is timeless. You can easily imagine spouses saying it to each other years and years from now.

A highly educated relative of mine (*though not my wife, Rebecca, who is also highly educated, and smarter than me*) has speculated that it might have come from Lucretius. But it's well-known that horned Lucretius, in his outlandish red outfit, brandishing a trident, is evil, while "I'm wrong. I'm sorry. I love you" is noble, progressive – designed to get folks closer together, not rend them apart.

Oh, that's *Lucifer* in that red outfit! Not Lucretius.

I apologize. I do that a lot, confuse the devil with old Romans.

I'll admit to you I was wrong, making that mistake. I'll say I'm sorry to you. But I won't say I love you, unless you're emotionally close to me.

And I don't expect you to say it to me. We probably don't even know each other. If I did know you I probably would like you. People who read my stuff are all likeable, assuming they paid for the book, and didn't just borrow from the library.

AM I PARTICULARLY QUALIFIED TO WRITE THIS BOOK?

My stepdaughter, after reading this section, asserted the list of my qualifications (*provided below*) could be severely cut, and the section include just two new, brief sentences:

> I once was married.
> Then I got divorced. (*This was pre-Rebecca*)

While she has a point, there are several other reasons which make me qualified. Here are some:

I once had occasion to visit a marriage counselor
I have a Ph.D. in Psychology
I am a college professor
I often do or say things to important people in my life which they think (no doubt mistakenly) I'm wrong about
I've done a little consumer research on the issue
I'm smart
I'm interested in the topic

And MOST important ---

I'M A GUY! (*Do you really want to take the advice of a girl on how you should act?*)

Here are some reasons why, in response, I'm *not* qualified:

While I once visited a marriage counselor, I personally am not a trained marriage counselor. (I went to one before my divorce, but I felt the 'counselor' that my wife-at-the-time chose for the two of us to see was a raging feminist who was very very angry at me because I was a man – and maybe because she wasn't. No way was she not taking sides.)

My Ph.D. in Psychology was in Social Psychology, not counseling or clinical. (Social psychologists, as the name implies, treat <u>whole societies</u>. We have much higher ambitions than those inefficient counseling and clinical psychologists whose practices concentrate on only one or two people at a time. While it's been many years since I've picked up a social psychology book, no less a journal in the literature, I still recall much of the material we studied. Like the famous Dakota studies by the esteemed social psychologist Festinger Milgram, who demonstrated that the inferiority residents of South Dakota felt was merely due to their state being below North Dakota on the map. His solution to the problem was ingenious – initiate an advertising campaign informing South Dakota residents that Nebraska residents were below them on the map. One reason this was ingenious was that this campaign led to a new client – the state of Nebraska.)

My professorship is in the Marketing Department of a university, and marketing is not a subject directly applicable to this issue, except in the sense that a person is always marketing themselves, even to their loved ones. And this manual is of special value when the loved one is on the opposite side of a rift.

How can you trust anyone who important people believe says lots of things that are wrong?

My consumer research is mostly conducted among my friends and acquaintances. Not to disparage these folks, but suppose I'm weird, and as a result have many weird friends and acquaintances with weird ideas, who are not at all typical of 'normal' folks. Though they may be typical of weirdos.

Yeah, I may be smart, but as my mother told me many times, "You may be smart in book-learning, but you don't have common sense."

While I am interested in the topic, what I really need is income to support my retirement. Though, come to think of it, I expect never to retire. So, forget about the retirement money, it's not that important. I just need to keep busy writing helpful books -- a good way to extend life for anyone.

No, thinking further on it, forget the forgetting of money. It *is* important.

So, now that I've presented both sides, illustrating a lack of any bias on my part, you'll need to decide if I'm qualified to write this manual.

But the most thorough method of managing this decision is to finish reading the book. Only then, judge my qualifications and determine for yourself if I'm brilliant or a fraud.

IS THIS BOOK ONLY FOR HUSBANDS AND STEADY BOYFRIENDS?

This book is about relationships. Relationships among folks close to one another. That is, you might tell a complete stranger you were *wrong* for stepping on their foot and *sorry* about it. But you wouldn't say, "I *love you*" to a stranger, would you? Unless they were *really* attractive and your mate wasn't nearby. (*Nah! Not even then. I was just kidding, Rebecca.*)

And, don't say it to your boss, unless either your wife is your boss at work (*in which case I pity you*), or your boss is someone you're having outside trysts with.

The saying, 'I'm wrong. I'm sorry. I love you' *can* apply to parents and children, siblings, and others you feel affection toward.

In this manual I'll just be referring to what husbands and boyfriends should do, since that's what's expected from the subtitle. (*'Getting along with your mate after a squabble. A survival manual for men.'*)

Nevertheless, lessons learned about wives and steadies can often be applied to other relationships as well.

So, don't set aside this book just because you don't have a steady or you're not married.

Also, because one day you might.

DO YOU REALLY NEED THIS BOOK?

Look, you're a guy. So, you're pretty sure you're never really really wrong about the reason for the squabble. Even if it's a bad argument instigated by you, there's usually a really really really good reason why you did or said something instigatory in the first place.

Ok, sometimes, but rarely, you screw up.

But even if you didn't, your mate may think you screwed up. So, either way – you screwing up, or your mate thinking you did even if you didn't – you need the advice in this book.

You know that at times there are things you do or say that bother her. But that's really her problem, isn't it?

Well, not really. It's not only her problem. Because if it's her problem, it's yours too. You're the one who has to live with her.

You're aware she has a problem in that she's too picky. (*She is a woman, after all.*) But that's now your problem because you have to deal with the fallout if you want to go forward smoothly with a satisfying relationship.

Remember, though, that you DON'T really want to *win* an argument with your mate.

Why?

Because that means *she loses*! Then (*depending on her disposition at the time*), there may be hell to pay!

Also, there are no doubt very good reasons to maintain that usually wonderful relationship you have with her.

Maybe she's an awesome trophy on your arm when you attend professional wrestling matches, or a superior cook, or a smart shopper. Maybe she has great nursing skills, is a superior housekeeper, a great back rubber, perhaps a wage earner to help support your living standard, a caring attentive mother.

And, to top it off, she's a wild and dexterous mattresser. (*I'd use the term 'whoopee maker', but the wife Rebecca says that term is outdated*).

Plus, your mate is a sympathetic listener after you've had a hard day (*on those few occasions when you want to talk about it*), and an accomplished conversationalist when her conversation doesn't revolve around your faults.

So, it's uncomfortable for you when her pickiness causes a squabble and ruins your day. There is tension about.

On the whole, relationships are more of a woman than a man thing. (*More about men vs. women later.*) Women think a lot about relationships. Men don't. Not most real men. But there are exceptions. For example, yours truly, the author of this savant manual.

Another exception, in the reverse, but this time on the distaff side, is the wife of my friend Barnaby Zill, Mrs. Zill, who thinks more about bon-bons than relationships.

Putting exceptions aside, women are better than men at managing relationships. Most guys are at a disadvantage when it comes to that. Women are somehow educated to manipulate men to do their bidding. As proof, didn't your mate manipulate you into getting together as a couple?

If you answered "No" that's just one example. She manipulated you into thinking that *you* made it all come about.

And that sort of control is another reason (*besides managing squabbles*) why you really need this book.

IS 'SURVIVAL' TOO STRONG A WORD?

Part of the subtitle of this book is 'A survival manual for men.'

But what is meant by 'survival'? And is 'survival' too strong of a word?

Obviously, if your mate wants to shoot you, this manual will not save your life. Unless somehow she misses and this book deflects the bullet intended for your brain (*or maybe more likely your groin*) and it ricochets back at her, the ingrate, so she can't fire another round.

And this book says nothing about her exiling you to the wild outdoors where you survive by:

- Befriending ferocious animals so they don't eat you

- Using *harmless* leaves as toilet paper instead of poison ivy

- Collecting rainwater and somehow adding fluoride found naturally in nature

- Lighting a fire without a match without singeing your body hair

- Finding edible acorns while avoiding vicious attacks by the squirrels who consider those acorns their lunch

- Preparing delicious insect stew

- Tossing a salad made from strange plants and wild la-la mushrooms

- Extracting yourself from quicksand

- Chasing off a wild boar by singing Row Row Row Your Boat falsetto (*Wild boars tend to run away from humans they think are crazy*)

Survival means a continued existence. But existence can be defined in other ways than not losing your life.

When I write about survival in this book I refer to the continued lifestyle (*hopefully happy, but at the least satisfactory*) the man is accustomed to, and his ability to outlast the fallout of a rift in a relationship with a love-interest woman.

Sometimes a man doesn't want to survive a rift and is pleasantly rewarded when an unhealthy relationship either explodes or dissipates, either way disappearing. The final breakup is welcome.

If that seems to be the case with you, if you don't care to stay in this relationship any more, then maybe you should do the opposite of what this manual advises.

On the other hand, most often a man wants the relationship to continue, and in a mentally healthy way. He wants that relationship to survive, to continue its existence, and even more, to thrive.

That's what this book is about – helping a man continue to be happy and healthy in the aftermath of a tiff, spat, or squabble with his mate. So, in that sense this book is, in its way, about survival training.

And so, 'survival' is not too strong of a word.

PAY ATTENTION TO PUNCTUATION

The speech promoted in this manual has seven words: I'm – Wrong – I'm – Sorry – I - Love – You.

It also has periods after certain of the words. So, the speech, when putting the words and punctuation together becomes:

> I'm wrong.
> I'm sorry.
> I love you.

A lesson for you: When you say these words, make sure your punctuation is clearly and accurately placed. Don't forget to insert the periods in their proper position.

For example, one poor gentleman approached his wife after a squabble and said, "I'm wrong. I'm sorry I love you." (*No period after 'sorry.'*)

She took his speech to mean what he just said -- that he was sorry that he loved her. She intuited that he wished that he didn't love her, and was wrong about ever being with her in the first place.

You can see how she could react to what he said, can't you? Especially when she was already upset with him for his sin of bringing home the wrong percentage of reduced fat milk.

This faux pas turned what had been a mere squabble into an argument, and since they lived in a community property state, he lost half his house. They now live separately, he in the east portion, she in the west portion. (*They uneasily share the kitchen and the front entrance.*)

Along with the punctuation, make sure you place the words in the proper order. Another example. A man (*maybe someone just like you*), started his speech to his wife after a mere tiff, with, "I'm sorry I was wrong."

She understood that he was being sarcastic. He wasn't apologizing for being incorrect, but that he was just sorry that the whole shebang happened so the sex-crazed bastard could get his dose of mattressing.

She wanted to hear him say he was wrong. Period.

Now you might ask, "What about commas? Are they equally effective as periods?"

The answer is that yes, commas can be equally effective for purposes of our speech, except after the word 'love.'

Punctuation Rule #33: Don't end a sentence with a comma.

ARE SEVEN WORDS THE RIGHT AMOUNT?

As mentioned earlier, the expression 'I'm wrong. I'm sorry. I love you' has exactly seven words. But is it possible to delete words or add words to make the message more powerful?

Obviously, if your lucky number is seven, and you cling to it intensely you're going to say no. Unless, of course, you add a word for each word deleted, leaving it at seven.

However, most people have lucky numbers other than seven which they use to control their lives. Which is silly. If you're going to run your life based on a lucky number it's gotta be seven.

But does it really make sense to run your love life on the basis of lucky numbers? Even the number seven? Maybe financial decisions, but not your love life.

So don't use the magical expression just because it has seven words. In fact, you might consider using more or fewer words.

Fewer Words

Brevity is usually better than lengthity in expressing oneself, as long as the intended meaning gets across. So let's see what happens when we delete certain words from "I'm wrong. I'm sorry. I love you."

There are hundreds of ways to delete words, even when there are just seven of them. To an extreme, you can delete *all* the words, which obviously means you've said nothing.

That's pointless! Duh!

Or, you can delete six words, which means there is just one word you say to her. Let's see.

Suppose you went to her and said, with great economy, "I'm"?

"What?" she'd ask.

"I'm."

"I'm what?"

"I'm."

You sound pretty moronic, don't you, just repeating "I'm." (*This on top of the moron she may already think you are by causing the rift in the first place.*)

Now, you'd really never just say "I'm," of course. Obviously you know you need to add words to that one. But which words would you add?

You could add two more words from the expression, such as – 'I'm,' and 'I.' So now you're saying to her, "I'm. I'm. I." But that's not much better than just 'I'm'.

Your one word, of course, can be another of the expression's words. 'Sorry,' for example. That's better than 'I'm'. But if you go to her and say, 'Sorry' she might misinterpret your intentions and think you are merely sorry that you're at odds (*and not because you did something wrong*). Or, even worse, that you think she is just a pitiful person. (*At this point, ever since your schism, she's ready to think the worst of you.*)

Same thing if you approach her and say just, 'Ial.' She may very well think you're accusing her of being wrong.

You could say several of the key words to her, like, "Wrong. Sorry. Love." But she might construe that you're saying that *she* is wrong, that *she* is a sorry person, and you love it when she's wrong. (*Again, her interpretation is colored by her current negative attitude toward you.*)

At any rate, there are hundreds of ways of reducing the number of words in the magical expression. I think you'll agree that 'I'm wrong. I'm sorry. I love you,' the basic seven words, is the most economical way of getting across the message you want to.

So, let's rule out deleting any of the seven magical words. And if you think you've just wasted your time reading this Fewer Words section, you're probably correct. I'm wrong. I'm sorry. (*But I don't love you, unless you're my family.*)

Silly dilly me!

BUT DO GO ON TO THE NEXT SECTION.

Adding Words

There are numerous ways of adding words to the expression, 'I'm wrong. I'm sorry. I love you.'

But how many words should be added? And which ones?

Obviously I cannot deal with all the possibilities. They are theoretically infinite. Especially if you include words in a foreign language. But let's examine some which may seem reasonable.

For example, how about placing enhancers before key words in the expression? An example:

'I'm profoundly wrong. I'm inordinately sorry. I thoroughly love you.'

This may sound good initially. But it's very easy for her to decide this is overkill, and you're being overly melodramatic about what amounts to no more than a squabble. These are words used after an argument, not a squabble. Now she thinks there's something you've done beyond the cause of the original squabble. Your previous behavior is even worse than she thought. What you've just said enhances the seriousness of it all.

Or, she may think you're being sarcastic. (*Remember, her interpretation is colored by her current negative attitude toward you.*)

So, my suggestion is not to go overboard in the modifiers you use.

Another possibility is to add an endearment after you say, "I love you." This will be covered in the next section of this manual.

SHOULD YOU ADD ANYTHING AFTER THE WORDS "I LOVE YOU"?

If you really want to reconnect with your wife or steady, add something to the 'I love you.'

One example is to add her first *and* middle names. Many women find this extremely sexy.

That is, tell her, "I'm wrong. I'm sorry. I love you, Betty Lou."

Obviously, to avoid getting into worse trouble, be sure her first and middle names are Betty Lou, and in that order.

Another option is to add a title to the phrase, before her name. For example, "I'm wrong. I'm sorry. I love you, *Ms.* Betty." (*Or even better, Ms. Betty Lou.*)

Of course, she may reply "I love you, *Mr.* Carmine," which you really don't care for because you don't want to be thought of as a hairdresser, and, even worse, your name isn't Carmine.

If your mate is a professor, be wary of using her title. If you say, "I'm wrong. I'm sorry. I love you, *Professor* Betty," she may think you're being sarcastic and really calling her a know-it-all. This is true whether she's a professor or not.

Of course, still another option is to add at the end of 'I love you' the endearing nickname you usually call her. Most couples have words of endearment for each other.

I asked a bunch of friends and associates which endearments they used. In many cases they were the some old tired ones – Honey, Sweetheart, Babe, Darling, Cutie-Pie, Doll, Sugar, Sweetie, Your Highness.

There were also more singular ones, like my favorites, Little Cougar, Mrs. God, and Honeypooperlambchop.

For example, "I'm wrong. I'm sorry. I love you, Little Cougar."

(This might be said no matter what your age in relation to hers.)

If you have no endearments with your mate, or use only the old tired uncreative standbys, it may pay for you to increase your endearment vocabulary.

Following shortly are some endearments supplied by the folks I surveyed. (*Most can go either way – men calling women and women calling men, such as 'My Little Sex Toy,' or 'Sweetiepiehead.' And some would just go in one direction, such as women calling their male mate, 'Such A Good Daddy.' Or men calling their female mate, 'Mama Marshmallow.'*)

Even more endearments can be found on Wikipedia -- the true source of complete and absolutely, undeniably accurate info about anything.

But the endearments presented I know were *actually used* by real people. (*Of course I promised them anonymity, though they may be weirdos because they're somehow associated with me.*)

Feel free to adopt any of them.

Angel
Angelface
Babe
Babycakes
Babydoll
Babyhead
Babypoo
Babylox
Battering Ram
Beauty
Belle of My
  Heart
Berry Crumble
Big Guy
Booger
Bubala
Bugs
Butt Beauty
Cookie
  Monster
Cuddlebuns
Cutie Pie
Da Man
Darling
Deliciousness
Dirty Little
  Girl
Doll
Doll Face
Doofus
Dreamboat
Dude
Dudette
Funny Face
Gorgeous
Grab Bag

Grabmeister
Heartbreaker
Hey Schlomo
Honey
Honey Bunch
Honey Pie
Honeypoo
Honeypooper-
  lambchop
Hot Lady
Hot-and-
  Horny
Hot Stuff
Hubby
Juice Machine
Kitten
Lemon Cake
Little Butt
Little Cougar
Little Hottie
Lochinvar
Longman
Love Bug
Love
Lover
Lovey
Lovums
Lucky
Mama Marsh-
  mallow
Midnight
  Rider
Milfy
Miss Beaver

Mon Petit
  Chou
  (*French*)
Moochie
Moonbeam
Mrs. God
Muffin
Muffy
Mule
My Beautiful
  Bride
My Bunny
My Everything
My Little
  Keeper
My Love
Mr. Man
My Little
  Cabbage
My Little Sex
  Toy
My Little
  Tiffany
  Girl
My Sex
  Machine
Pattycake
Peanut
Pookie
Pookieface
Precious
Princess
Puffy Cheeks
Putchkala
Puzzle Piece

Pumpkin	Sugar	Tight-and-Tiny
Queen	Sugar Lips	Tiny Little Girl
Ratface	Sugar Pie	Tootsie
Schnookums	Sugarplum	Tubby Wubby
Sexpot	Sweetcheeks	Twerp
Sexy Little Thing	Sweetheart	Twinkle Toes
Sexy Mexi	Sweetpea	Wifey
Silly Pot	Sweetie Pie	Your Highness
Skinny Minny	Sweetiepie-head	You Sweet Thing You
Slow & Easy	Sweets	Young Thing
Spanky	Sweetums	Zinger
Spunky	Tatala	
Such a Good Daddy	Taut-and-Toned	
Sunshine	Ted (*his name was Melvin*)	
Slim	The Tongue	
Squish		
Strawberry Shortcake		

HINT:
To enhance the effectiveness of your speech, while you're saying your particular variation of 'I'm wrong. I'm sorry. I love you,' hold her hand and stare into her eyes. This'll enhance the illusion of genuineness.

It'll also work if you *are* actually genuine.

Which brings me to the next section of this manual.

DO YOU HAVE TO MEAN IT WHEN YOU SAY "I'M WRONG"?

You're admitting you're wrong for a reason -- to repair a glitch in your relationship, to relieve tension. Maybe you have a larger goal of wanting her to do something (*mattress?*), or allow you to do something that won't happen unless the squabble situation isn't in play.

So, when you say you are wrong, do you have to mean it?

Of course not!

Your mate may very well know that you never (*OK, rarely*) think you're wrong, and now you're 'Just saying it.' But still, the act of saying to her that you're wrong tells her that you are *trying* to work on the relationship, and that's good. So admitting you're wrong may be more powerful than you think.

And remember your mate probably wants to resolve the situation just as much as you do (*maybe even more if she's feeling like acting out her real hottie*). So, she'll no doubt easily buy into your overture, even if she sees right through you.

But whether you mean it or not, deliver it sincerely. Act genuine.

Not necessarily *be* genuine. Just act that way.

So, how does one <u>act</u> genuine when he is not really sincere?

Don't say you can't act! Everyone acts in real life. Even if you don't think you're acting. You already play different roles in life. You *act* differently when you're with your mate than when you're sloshed at the bar with your male friends. Or, you may be acting when you tell your mate she's prettier than her sister (*if she isn't*). It's not that hard to do, is it?

So, acting is something you've always done. Done all your life. You can do it now!!!

But beyond your normal acting in everyday life, if you've ever taken acting lessons you're ahead of the game. However, even if you haven't, and you don't quite feel ready to act genuine, you can take some learning from what actors do to prepare for a role.

Remember, actors are *acting* the role. They are not *really* the character they play. If there's a play or movie about Attila The Hun, somebody's got to play Attila. And unless there's reincarnation, it's not going to be the real Attila. (*Wouldn't it be a hoot if the real Attila had been reincarnated into the present day Dalai Lama?*)

The actor does not personally have to be anything like Attila. (*although it might be easier for him if he is.*)

There are three ways for actors to learn to become the character they play:

- Immerse themselves fully in the role so they actually 'become' the character they play

- Pretend they are the character, but not to the extent of *becoming* that character

- Copy the behavior, speech pattern, mannerisms, and so on, of the character they play, or someone like that character.

The first option, 'becoming' the genuine character you play, may not seem available to you in this current instance of a rift, But in fact it is. Just recall a prior time when you were genuine, and act as you did then. If it worked out well for you, let yourself relive that time. Become that person. What was your posture then? Your voice volume and tone? Your eye contact? The positions of your mouth when the other person was speaking? What you were doing with your hands? Was your fly zipped? If not, what were you doing with your hands?

Try to relive that conciliatory genuineness, like maybe the just after the time you tossed pennies at your high school algebra teacher when she complained about being underpaid? Or, when you had to explain to your girlfriend why it was necessary for her to take medication for that STD you accidentally gave her. (*Of course, if that girlfriend morphed into your current mate, maybe you should act slightly different from then, so it doesn't remind her of the earlier uncomfortable instance.*)

If that reliving situation didn't work out well, ask yourself why not? What mistakes did you make, like immodesty, dishonesty, disingenuousness, accusation? What would you have done differently?

But consider that even if your behavior was genuine then, if it was counterproductive at that time then it may not work out this time either. For example, if you genuinely got angry, and your accidental spit slobbered all over her face, you don't need to repeat that.

The second option, pretending, is like the first, but you're not fooling yourself into thinking you *are* the character. You know you're just pretending.

Maybe you can ask yourself why the character you're playing became the way he was. For example, if you're pretending to be playing Attila you might decide that Attila became the way he was because his strict teacher in Hunnic kindergarten kept rapping his knuckles with a ruler for making disparaging comments about Gothic gypsies.

In the third option, just *copying* the behavior of the character, you'd identify the character and replicate them as best you can. For example, Hitler might've learned to behave as he did when he watched that Charlie Chaplin movie about a dictator. Nowadays, a good actor of the right stature certainly can learn to play Hitler by either watching old Hitler movies (or newsreels), or that Charlie Chaplain movie.

If you copy well then you'll seem genuine. So just copy someone you know who acts genuine, whether they mean it or not.

And above all, when you address her, say it like a man. Assertive, strong, no groveling.

You are not a wimp!

IS IT WIMPY TO SAY YOU'RE WRONG AND SORRY?

I just finished a novel written by a woman. The story centered around the lives of two women with husbands. Very well written, sort of. Good twists. Nice metaphors. Just a few big words I didn't understand.

But it had a major flaw, as far as I was concerned, although it might not have been major, or a flaw at all, to women who read the book. The two husbands were constantly saying they were sorry to their wives. On just about every page the guys, who didn't even know each other, were telling their spouse they were sorry, virtually begging for forgiveness.

OK, there may have been good reason for them to be sorry; one husband had an affair with her best friend, and the other committed a murder of passion just because the woman he killed laughed at him.

But they came across as so so wimpy, apologizing every chance they got. And the author didn't seem to use any of the words that might be found in a thesaurus to replace 'sorry.' Over and over. In almost every sentence. I got sick of it. 'Sorry, sorry, sorry, sorry, sorry.' It made me sorry I was even reading that book. (*But I had to finish reading it to see if somewhere along the way one of the wives would have said, "Stop with the sorry business. Can't you just consult a thesaurus and use some different words to express your sorry feeling?" Neither of them ever did.*)

Now, maybe I can stomach one wimpy major male character per book. But not two. I began to disrespect the author.

At any rate, there is a possible danger in telling your mate that you are sorry. Just make sure you don't come across as wimpy.

Always remember that you are a man. And a man stands up for what he believes. You are not a wimp crawling back to his mate, pleading desperately for forgiveness, about to fall apart if she rebuffs your attempt to recapture that contented relationship.

So, when you deliver your 'I'm wrong. I'm sorry. I love you,' pay attention to *how* you are conveying the message. Consider your body language, your tone of voice, your gestures, your posture. Saying those charmed words doesn't have to be wimpy.

Don't cry or sob. Don't even have moist eyes.

Don't get down on your knees, pleading.

Don't assume a stance in such a way that you seem a subject to her royal queen.

Don't fail to show confidence, or seem that you are groveling, helpless. Say what you have to say with conviction. Expect your overture to work.

It's OK to look into her eyes, to take and hold her hand, as long as she realizes that you are not doing all this out of desperation.

After all, isn't one of the reasons she chose you in the first place that you are a real man (*OK, her caveman, to be somewhat politically incorrect*), who watches over and protects her? Even if she's physically stronger than you (*much like Mrs. Zill, who can TKO Barnaby*), doesn't she want that reassurance that you are her ultimate protector?

No?

All right, then. Sometimes the answer is 'No.'

If she's the dominant sort, who chose you because you are the submissive she always wanted, and she is the dominant you always wanted, then *do* grovel, cry, plead, and slavishly address her as 'Mistress,' just before you lick and kiss her high-heel booted toes.

If that's the type you want to be, go for it.

So, it's not necessarily wimpy to say, "I'm wrong. I'm sorry. I love you," unless you actually are a wimp.

WHICH IS BETTER TO SAY: 'I'M WRONG' OR 'YOU'RE RIGHT'?

Earlier, when discussing 'You're right' it was in the context of what you should say *beforehand* to avoid that rift. But now we need to address the 'You're right' in the context of the full expression, which ends with, 'I'm sorry. I love you.' This occurs when you've already had that squabble.

That is, some folks have suggested that, when you've already had that squabble and wish to resolve it, it's best to use the words, 'You're right,' instead of 'I'm wrong.'

(*Note that the remainder of the speech -- 'I'm sorry. I love you' -- is the same for both ways of apologizing, so let's put those words aside for now.*)

Others have said it doesn't make difference; that 'I'm Wrong' and 'You're Right' are two ways of saying the same thing.

I mean, if you are wrong, then it follows that she is right, no? Or, if she's right, you are wrong? Gotta be.

Much like heads and tails. If you toss a coin and it comes up heads then it's not tails. If it comes up tails, it's not heads. (*Of course there are the slim possibilities the coin lands on its side, or your inaccurate toss results it dropping into your underwear. Or hers. But the odds of any of those happening are greater than one in ten, so let's forget about them.*)

However, are 'I'm wrong' and 'You're right' the same in this arena of man-woman relationships? Is it true they have identical meanings, when it comes down to it?

Methinks not. They do differ.

In evaluating each alternative let's assume when you say, 'I'm wrong' or 'You're right' you present the idea genuinely and sincerely, and not from exasperation. *(That is, out of frustration with your mate nagging like a harridan, you spout argumentatively, "All right already! I'm wrong/You're right! I'm sorry. I love you.")*

According to an educated relative of mine, the first (*'I'm wrong'*) connotes the deficiency of the apologist. The second (*'You're right'*) the righteousness of the person being apologized to, the apologee.

Let's examine the connotations of each phrase. We'll start with the 'You're right.'

There are some very favorable aspects of beginning this way. For one, it's more flexible. 'You're right' is less apologetic than 'I'm wrong' in the sense that it may denote that she has a point which you can see, and her point trumps yours. BUT, your side isn't *completely* unfounded. You still have reasons why you aren't totally wrong. So, you save some face.

Also, 'You're right' uses a positive word – 'right' – while 'wrong' is a negative word. The use of the upbeat 'right' may brighten the atmosphere surrounding the whole situation, especially in the view of the apologee, who is complimented, rather than you, the apologist, who is flogging himself to some degree by saying, 'I'm wrong.'

On the other hand, let's assume 'I'm wrong' connotes the apologist's deficiency. Now, consider that the apologist (*e.g., you*) has decided to admit this. He has thought about it and is now willing to admit the wrongdoing. This admission has greater gravity than some other words you might have used (*such as 'You're right'*), obviously designed to appease her. Especially if the apologist rarely admits he's wrong. (*Is that you, reader?*)

As one woman I spoke with reported, "My husband never says he's wrong about anything. If he said he was I'd think something was wrong with his mental health. I'd be very concerned."

Such grave concern would naturally lead to any squabble being put in the background, or disappearing altogether. After all, how important can a squabble be when mental health might be at risk? So now, healing of the relationship has occurred because there may be good reason for her to be concerned. Maybe dementia is having an early onset.

Finding out that he has early dementia can have important benefits. She can enroll him in yoga and meditation classes. (*On second thought, she might not want to enroll him because those classes mostly consist on women in tighties, and if he starts to hit on any of his classmates he can blame it on his dementia, and do it again the next time and the times after that because he forgot she told him not to.)*

Another thing she can do to stem advance of his dementia is, as queen of the kitchen, to place him on a healthy luscious diet of milk thistle, quinoa, and bok choy – all smothered in krill oil, and seasoned with turmeric and cumin.

At any rate, him saying, 'I'm wrong' may end up being a very good happenstance.

Now, there are some situations where a man might say "You're right" which have nothing to do with any form of dispute. Like if you ask, "Where's the orange juice in the fridge?" She says, "It's in the back, behind the 2% reduced fat milk."

You then look where directed, find the o.j., and tell her, "You're right." No conflict there. (*Unless she follows up by again pointing out your error in buying the 2% reduced fat milk rather than the 1% she requested.*)

So, 'You're right' sometimes lacks in heavy significance. 'I'm wrong' has much greater gravity.

Considering all this, is one better than the other? Is 'I'm wrong' more effective than 'You're right'?

It may depend on your particular situation and who you are and what your mate is like. For some 'I'm wrong' may be more effective, while for others it's 'You're right'.
Of course, you can use both phrases. For example, tell her, "You're right. I'm wrong" as a preface to "I'm sorry. I love you."

Hmmm.

But that may be overkill.

Also, it might indicate that *you think* she is more interested in proving you wrong than her being right about the particular instance which caused the squabble in the first place. (*Of course, this may be correct, but you don't want to bring it up. It'll end in another squabble. Or maybe even a quarrel, no less an argument.*)

Still, I'm not going to change the book title from, "I'm Wrong. I'm Sorry. I Love You" to the less catchy and more verbose, "You're Right. I'm Wrong. I'm Sorry. I Love You."

What about, "You're Right. I'm Sorry. I Love You" as a title?

It may exist seemingly a toss-up, but not categorically. For some intrepid logic the 'Wrong' term in the title fashions this book to appear more waggish, and most of the populace would preferably be engrossed in perusing a tome with a comedic attitude toward disharmonic conflict than a more serious pedantic dissertation.

See, I told you I, your author, was a college professor! I had to get in some content illustrating my academic proficiency. Did so in the prior paragraph! Good job, huh?

Now that I've demonstrated my qualifications as a member of the academic community, let me rephrase the paragraph to make it easier to understand.

It may appear a 50-50 proposition, but not really. For some reason the 'Wrong' word makes this book seem more comedic, and most people would rather read a book with a funny slant than a serious one.

Yes, people do judge a book by its cover, despite brainy librarians smugly advising against it. Judging a book by its cover means deciding on its worth before reading it. (*It's stupid to judge a book by its cover if you've already read it. Duh!*) Since the title of this manual is clearly printed on the cover, that rule, "Judge a book by its cover," should apply here as well. And 'Wrong' is funnier than 'Right.' People can't help being drawn to funny. Thus, 'Wrong' is more likely to engage reader purchase interest, says consumer researcher me.

Moreover, someone admitting they're wrong is so infrequent-- who *wants* to say they're wrong?--, that it's fascinating and intriguing. Saying you're wrong is a much more powerful hook than saying someone else is right.

Another reason I'm not changing the title is that you've already bought this book which has the title, "I'm Wrong. I'm Sorry. I Love You." And I'm not coming to your home to replace the cover. Even if you offer me lobster and bouillabaisse.

WHEN TO SAY AND NOT TO SAY 'I'M WRONG'

There are two types of situations where you should admit you're wrong:

- You *are* wrong and it's obvious you are
- You aren't wrong but it's in your best interests to say you are

My stepdaughter, when reviewing a draft of this chapter, said, "Obviously only the second type is realistic." But I'm sure she was just being facetious, since no woman thinks any man is faultless.

It's foolish to constantly deny that you are wrong. Even if you think you are never wrong, you're not. (*You never really, really, really think you're wrong, do you?*) You are not perfect. No one is ever perfect.

And even if you were perfect you'd want to admit you were wrong some of the time, and not carry yourself as if you're some flawless god. Otherwise, people will hate you.

And your lack of modesty would in fact flaw you, so you won't be flawless or perfect anyway.

So, to retain your image as a reasonable, likeable human being it's OK to admit that you aren't perfect by saying, "I'm wrong" at least every once in a while.

Even if you know definitely, for sure, that you are *not* wrong about some issue you've rifted on with your significant other, it might pay for you to say you're wrong if doing so impacts favorably on your health, wallet, or relationship.

Here's a chart to help you decide whether or not to *admit* you're wrong in different types of situations.

The chart has three components.

One component is whether the conflict is Major, Minor, or somewhere in the Middle. This is really a continuum, but for sake of simplicity, we'll make it three categories – Major, Middle, and Minor. (*While I've indicated earlier that this book does not really deal with Major conflicts, I thought I'd throw it into this part of the discussion.)*

The second is whether you were actually, factually Wrong OR actually, factually Not Wrong. Just two levels. An example of definite Wrong would be when you were mattressing with a person other than your significant other (*without her permission*).

In addition to occasions where you did not misbehave, the Not Wrong would include matters of opinion where you aren't wrong since it's just opinion, especially if her opinion is wrong.

The third component also has two levels – Caught or Not Caught. Caught refers to whether your mate has actually caught you doing something wrong. Like you were naked, mattressing with a person other than your significant other (*without her permission, of course*) and your mate just happened to open the bedroom door. Or, on a more minor note, that you bought 1% reduced fat milk, instead of 2%. Or, maybe even worse, you bought 2% reduced fat milk, instead of 1%.

The fourth column in the chart deals with whether you should *admit* you were wrong. The answer depends on the information in the prior three columns.

LEVEL OF RIFT	ACTUALLY WRONG	CAUGHT OR NOT	WHAT YOU SHOULD DO
MAJOR	**WRONG**	**CAUGHT**	**ADMIT**
MAJOR	NOT WRONG	NOT CAUGHT	DON'T ADMIT
MAJOR	WRONG	NOT CAUGHT	DON'T ADMIT
MAJOR	NOT WRONG	NOT CAUGHT	DON'T ADMIT
MIDDLE	**WRONG**	**CAUGHT**	**ADMIT**
MIDDLE	NOT WRONG	NOT CAUGHT	OK TO ADMIT
MIDDLE	WRONG	NOT CAUGHT	OK TO ADMIT
MIDDLE	NOT WRONG	NOT CAUGHT	OK TO ADMIT
MINOR	**WRONG**	**CAUGHT**	**ADMIT**
MINOR	NOT WRONG	NOT CAUGHT	OK TO ADMIT
MINOR	WRONG	NOT CAUGHT	OK TO ADMIT
MINOR	NOT WRONG	NOT CAUGHT	OK TO ADMIT

In some cases you should admit, in some cases you shouldn't, and in other cases it's optional, a gray area, something you decide on a case by case basis depending on the situation details and how much like a rhinoceros you feel at the moment. (*My stepdaughter thinks the word 'horny' is outdated and creepy, so instead I used rhinoceros. I considered using moose, or bighorn sheep, but a rhinoceros has a bigger horn than both of those. And a rhino has just one horn, and visually... well you know. And I'm talking about a dexterous gentle rhino here, not a clunky one.*)

ADMIT and DON'T ADMIT are clear directives.

OK TO ADMIT refers to your option to say "I'm wrong" or not. You can go either way.

So, you'll see you'll want to admit you were wrong whenever you've been *caught* being wrong. (*Well, maybe not want to admit, but be forced by reality to do so.*) This can range from buying the incorrect percentage of reduced fat milk (*the container sitting right there as proof*) to being caught naked in bed with someone other than your mate.

Defending yourself by asserting you're not wrong when you've clearly been caught is not only lame, but questions your whole integrity.

But sometimes you might want to admit to being wrong, even if you don't *think* you're wrong, or even if you *know* you're not wrong, because such an admission will enhance your relationship. For example, in the case of a minor tiff, you've got little to lose, and you may gain a surprise mattressing.

To help you along in your quest for implementing admission strategies, here are some additional examples of *minor* tiffs, matters on which some couples have had disputes:

You put too much garlic in the Jello

You didn't put down the toilet seat after using it

You forgot it was the sixth anniversary of the finalization of her first divorce

You threw away yesterday's newspaper which had a 10 cent coupon for her favorite laxative

You left a smidgeon of schmutz when you washed the pot

You neglected to buy her a greeting card for President's Day

You left a drip after you finished your shower

You strongly asserted that (insert name) should not have won the Academy Award for best sound grip in a documentary, while she disagreed with your choice

You emptied the dishwasher and put all the dishes away, but the dishwasher had never been turned on

The recording you bought of the greatest song hits of Queen didn't include Bohemian Rhapsody

You watered her artificial paper flowers

You inserted the toilet tissue on the roller facing the wrong way (as far as she was concerned)

I won't list reasons for the more *major* arguments, since, not only did I say earlier that this manual only covers minor offenses, but also because some of these major ones may be very tempting and might ruin your life if you're caught behaving that way.

OK, I give in. Or, maybe I can't resist. Here are a few reasons that may lead to arguments: (*Note: Some may have been cited earlier.*)

Having a mattress affair with someone not your mate

Gambling away your life savings shooting craps in Vegas

Quitting your high paying job in order to become a professional ice-fisherman

Posting nude photos of your mate on your Facebook page

Bringing home a mature St. Bernard dog to live with you two in your small apartment

Photo shopping her face onto a full-body nude photo of Rosie O'Donnell and tweeting it out

Not putting the toilet seat down after using it. (This has now evolved into a major error -- even though it's under the minor ones listed earlier -- because you're still not putting it down after she's asked you a hundred times.)

Inviting over a male porno actor for dinner with you two, and then excusing yourself to leave for a business meeting. (Actually, she might like it. So, forget it is on this list.)

Having diarrhea at night whilst in the bed you two share and not getting up because you're having such a terrific dream

Celebrating loudly when her favorite team <u>loses</u> the championship game

You forgetting her name when she came over to be introduced while you were talking to a total honey you'd just met at a party

She wanting her mother to move in with you

She claiming to have talked with God at precisely 5 PM earlier that day, and you know that's impossible because God was already conversing with you precisely at 5 PM, and there's only one God. (On the other hand, He is all-powerful, so maybe it could happen. BTW, your mate might refer to God as "SHE is all-powerful." But we guys know for sure that God is male, don't we?)

She wanting to institutionalize you for dementia (or vice versa), perhaps for thinking God speaks directly with you

HOW SHOULD YOU DELIVER
"I'M WRONG. I'M SORRY. I LOVE YOU"?

Let's say you're at home, but in a different room than your mate with whom you've had a recent squabble, and now you decide to deliver the "I'm wrong" spiel. But how?

Should you call her on her cell? Or write it and get the missive to her? Or personally go in the room where she is and hand her the written message, or just say it?

You consider the possibilities…

Smart Phone
Calling her cell to deliver the message is silly. Why tie up both your line and hers?

Plus the reception on cell phones isn't the best, and in a situation like this you don't want to say, "*What?*" over and over. (*Especially when the 'what' you say or she says may be taken as incredulity over what's the other has said.* WHAT!)

And what about using minutes you have to pay for if you go over them? On both phones, no less.

So, scratch the smart phone alternative.

Write
If you decide to *write* you have options.

You can write it on a sheet of *paper* and leave it in a place she'll likely discover it. But that'll prolong the tension until that time she finds it. And what happens if gravy gets on it, and now, in addition to thinking you behaved poorly earlier, she now suspects you're a slob?

Or maybe just confirms what she already knows.

You can *email* it. But if she's really angry she may set her device to direct all your communications into spam, which she rarely checks or deletes robotically without checking.

Plus, an email message may be seen as cowardly, impersonal, absent of your handwriting. Although it is sort of handwriting in that there is a record it was sent from your email account.

You can *text* message. This might lighten the mood between you two once she receives it (*thinking, "How cute and clever of him, playing with me, recognizing how much I love to receive text messages"*), until she learns that you were serious in sending the message in that manner.

Again, text isn't your personal handwriting. But still handwriting of a sort, with your cell phone the device sending the message.

Still, what about the cost of the megabytes if you don't have unlimited texting? On both phones, no less.

One aspect of writing your apologetic message is that she isn't obliged to respond immediately. She can mull over her reply.

Then, she has the same options you just had, the same alternatives to go through mentally – phone, write, or in-person. This normal evaluation process may bring forth a sense of togetherness, as you mutually (*though independently*) decide to discuss the communication process you've needed to decide on – choosing among the same alternatives.

It's something you can share, a mutual experience of decision-making. A commonality of endeavor. A bonding of sorts.

But then again, this can prolong the tension caused in the original squabble, maybe even worsening as it festers over time.

And like handwriting, sending a message by email or text message yields a permanent behavioral record, an objective hard evidence of confession of malfeasance, something that might be significant, which she can point to at some future time, maybe even flaunting it to others, embarrassing you mightily. Or raise it in divorce court.

Of course, given this possibility of providing hard evidence, your mate may be impressed by your willingness to create evidence of your poor behavior because you have a desire to heal your mutual relationship.

Another option is to write your message and hand the paper to her. But then you're subject to her retort, "What, you haven't got a mouth?"

Verbally In Person
You can also say it verbally – just come out have those words emanate from your mouth, "I'm wrong. I'm sorry. I love you". Delivering the admission verbally in-person has some authority, a connotation of personal responsibility not present in a chicken-hearted written effort.

However, you'll need to be prepared for personal on-the-spot rejection and/or a long-winded discussion concerning why you did or said what you did and why it won't happen in the future. If your significant other is a witch or ogress you may leave yourself open to be beaten up verbally if not physically (*the latter if you were married to Mrs. Zill*).

Which Way Is Best?
So, in the end, what's the best way to say, "I'm wrong. I'm sorry. I love you"?

Phone? Nah, already scrapped! A written message? In-person?

When this question was posed to folks I surveyed the answer was overwhelming. A typical response was, "What are you nuts, you schmuck? Of course the best way is to say it in person. And you call yourself a student of human behavior? You're a psychologist?"

But you don't have to always follow the crowd.

It's not just me who doesn't have to. You too!

That's good psychological advice.

WHAT IF SHE MAKES THE ADMISSION AT THE SAME TIME AS YOU?

(Earlier I identified the two chapters of this manual which I thought were most important. Now, to be fair, I should point out that the current chapter is probably one of the least important. I mean, how often does it happen that two people meeting start to say the exact same thing to each other at the same exact time? Not very! But it could happen. And in the interest of thoroughness I'm covering it here. So you'll always be prepared. Just in case.)

Let's face it. When you say, "I'm wrong. I'm sorry. I love you" it's not out of any burning desire per se to admit you're wrong and sorry. The reason you do it is to repair a meaningful, satisfying relationship. You want to be back where you were before, getting along with your mate.

Now, isn't it logical that your mate might feel the same way as you do – wanting to heal the relationship?

Isn't that wonderful – you both have a desire to patch things up. Mutual motivation toward the same end!

What could go wrong?

Plenty!

So you go to her, or she goes to you, or you happen to meet in some middle place, which doesn't even have to be the bedroom.

One possibility is that you start your pitch, 'I'm wrong...' and at *exactly the same time* she starts the same pitch (*she having somehow gotten hold of this manual*), stating, "I'm wrong."

Neither of you gets very far before recognizing this overlapping. So, she begins to giggle, while you chuckle (*since real men don't giggle and real women don't chuckle*).

So, then you both stop, and you, as a courteous guy, play the 'ladies first' card and let her start.

But, knowing what she's going to say, once she offers, "I'm wrong," then in anticipation of what she's about to say, you chime in, finishing her speech for her, "You're sorry. You love me."

You think, of course, she'll appreciate the two of you being simpatico, you knowing her so well that you think alike. But no, she gets mad at you for interrupting, or maybe just because you're right in anticipating what she was going to say. So, she changes her tune. She corrects you, "No, I was going to say that I was wrong about ever being with you in the first place. Jerk!"

Wow! That didn't work.

So, instead, suppose you take a different approach. You let her finish her speech. "I'm wrong. I'm sorry. I love you." Then, you tell her you accept her apology. But now she's upset at you for making her into the bad guy (*excuse me, the bad person*) causing the schism, when she knew all along *you* were.

If she had let *you* finish the speech you would be the bad person. So now she thinks you tricked her into going first by seeming to be the gentleman. Now she resents you for being smarter than she is, and suddenly you have anything from a new tiff to an argument to deal with.

Wow! That didn't work either.

So, there are a couple of options you have left.

One is that after she completes her spiel, you having let her go first, you tell her you were going to say the same thing to her.

This may be sufficient to accomplish your goal of reconciliation.

Or, it's possible that she now withdraws her assertion about herself, and agrees with you that *you* were wrong all along, and *you* should be sorry. This really isn't a poor outcome, of course, since you were going to say this anyway. And she may be amused, having resolved the situation.

Another option is that you don't take the gentlemanly 'ladies first' approach, and you insist on saying the full 'I'm wrong. I'm sorry. I love you' instead of her. That would work!

So maybe the safest situation is for you to initiate the full admission, talking fast, before she gets a chance to talk, and hope she won't begin talking her admission at the same time you do.

Especially if it's a mere tiff that stands between you.

BE JUDICIOUS

I asked a number of women how they'd respond if their mate told them after a squabble, "I'm wrong. I'm sorry. I love you."

To some, there's the aspect of her feeling triumphant, having bragging rights (*though if she's smart she'll restrain herself from outright bragging*). Her mate has tapped out (*to use an MMA term – MMA the acronym for Mixed Martial Arts. Though hopefully, your rift will never get to that physical point.*).

Most women will feel more conciliatory toward her mate upon his admission. And maybe the whole squabble thing will be resolved. But then, the more cynical women will try to obtain complete closure on the issue causing the rift in the first place. That is, they'll add something like the dreaded, "What are we going to do about this so it won't ever happen again?"

OK, now that you've got to deal with her question, you can handle it in different ways. Here are some:

- Pretend you didn't hear the question and then change the subject

- Jump in and simply change the subject *before* she ever gets to ask the question

- Just after she asks the question, or maybe even just before she gets a chance to ask it, repeat 'I love you,' kiss her lightly on the cheek, give her a wink, and walk away

- Go into a wildly dissembled long dissertation to the point where she ultimately forgets she ever asked you the question

- Promise to not do or say what you did or said before. This is the easy way out. But what if you know you were right, and you very well *will* do or say it again in a comparable situation? Is it OK to lie, or not keep your promise? Only you can answer that question. Not up to me to make that judgment for you, reflecting on your character.

However you do it, remember, you've got to be prepared, must have a plan, just in case she asks the question.

A short time after I asked women how they'd react the *first* time they heard the phrase 'I'm wrong. I'm sorry. I love you' I asked those same women how they'd react if *a few weeks later*, on a different issue, her mate *again* said exactly, "I'm wrong. I'm sorry. I love you."

Most women would react along the lines of thinking, "Hmmm. This sounds like something you said before." And maybe she'd even tell him that. But she'd let it go, since it allowed her to feel triumphant again. And gave her a feeling of being loved, which most people want, even if it means ignoring the obvious.

But what would happen if her mate tried it a *third* time. The reaction –"Uh-uh! Same trick as before. Lame!" (*Of course if you have an observant but cynical mate you might get this reaction the second time it was said.*)

What does this suggest about what you should be doing as a transgressor? Or at least as a person who wants to make-up? (*Which may lead to make-out, to point to the obvious.*)

It means you may not be able to say the same old, "I'm wrong. I'm sorry. I love you" more than twice to the same person in a relatively short time period, unless the person has dementia and forgets what you said before. (*In that case you can say it as many times as you want.*)

You need an alternate mea culpa speech.

So, don't make the mistake of using, "I'm wrong. I'm sorry. I love you," too often. Be judicious in the rate of implementing that magical speech. Otherwise your mate will see right through you, at the very least become suspicious and distrusting, perhaps causing a new squabble.

With some exceptions (*addressed later*) using the statement thrice is probably the ultimate max, with twice more likely the max, at least within a relatively short time period.

So, be very prudent. For example, a consideration for some men is that they should save their, "I was wrong, I'm sorry, and I love you" for when they feel really really like a rhinoceros. (*The animal explanation was provided earlier.*)

Now, what can you say if you've reached your max?

To help you along, follow me. I've devised a way to present the same thoughts as before, but utilizing different words. Using my trusty thesaurus, I copied synonyms for the key words in the speech – wrong, sorry, love. Here they are:

WRONG

Incorrect	Criminal	Harm
Mistaken	Unethical	Damage
Erroneous	Amiss	Insult
Off beam	Unsuitable	Injustice
Wide of the mark	Improper	Offence
	Inappropriate	Offense
Immoral	Incorrect	Insult
Wicked	Sin	Ill-treat
Dishonest	Crime	Abuse
Illegal	Injury	Offend
Iniquitous	Wound	

SORRY

Apologetic	Unhappy	Pathetic
Regretful	Wretched	Poor
Remorseful	Miserable	Rueful
Repentant	Pitiful	
Sad	Forlorn	

LOVE

Darling	Tenderness	Worship
Dear	Feeling	Fancy
Dearest	Fondness	Like
Sweetheart	Devotion	Enjoy
Honey	Passion	Appreciate
Affection	Ardor	
Adoration	Amity	
Friendship	Adore	

So, now there are multiple ways for you to present the same message, but using some different words than the worn out (*in your now particular case*), 'I'm wrong. I'm sorry. I love you.'

Just take one word from each grouping -- WRONG, SORRY, LOVE -- and put them together.

For example, you might approach your mate and admit, "I was amiss. I'm regretful. I fancy you."

Or, "I was erroneous. I'm remorseful. I have amity toward you."

Or, "I was wide of the mark. I'm poor. I have fondness for you."

Whoops, that last one's just not quite correct. What's screwed up is that the word 'poor' is a synonym for 'sorry' only in certain applications of 'sorry.' As in, "You are a sorry excuse for a manual writer." So, let me adjust that last admission to, "I was wide of the mark. I'm *apologetic*. I have fondness for you."

If you're a good with numbers, you can figure out there are thousands and thousands of different combinations to get across the wrong, sorry, love message. And if you're not so good with figures, just take my word for it.

Or take the word of Barnaby Zill, my magnificent arithmetician friend, who in his brilliant doctoral thesis computed the value of pi to six quadrillion digits. (*It was brilliant because none of the professors on his doctoral thesis committee wanted to spend the time to check his work to see if he was correct. As his main advisor commented while handing Barnaby his doctoral diploma, "It would take a trillion years to go through all those numbers to see if you're right."*)

The incredibly hard-working and devoted to his projects Barnaby had already used up his quota of "I'm wrong. I'm sorry. I love you" speeches to his wife when she complained, "While you were computing all those digits our son grew up and just graduated college."

To which Barnaby asked, "We have a son?"

When his wife's eyes turned ablaze Barnaby realized he needed another version of apology if he wanted to keep her. Thinking quickly, and having committed the thesaurus to memory, his mind now put together his alternate version, "I was incorrect. I'm rueful. I like you."

But he didn't say it right away, since he was mulling over if he really wanted to keep his wife. After two hours he reached the end of his mull and decided he would (*after all she was a great cook*), and he delivered those sweet words, "I was incorrect. I'm rueful. I like you."

Worked like a charm!

Because there is a practical limitation on the number of times you can directly use the 'wrong, sorry, love' combination, and you may be reluctant to use the synonymistic substitutions, you may have to resort to a longer recitation, citing the specifics of what you were wrong and sorry about, and how much you love her.

So, here's an example of what a reasonable husband (*again Barnaby Zill*) once told his wife concerning a *minor* tiff:

I don't know how I could have made the calamitous, dreadful, mistake of buying 2% reduced fat milk instead of the 1% you requested. A mistake you never would have made if you had gone shopping, which you have understandably been reluctant to do ever since your plea bargain for shoplifting. Another weakness of mine is that I never understood why you didn't drink nonfat if you wanted to lose all that flab. But lack of knowledge is my continuing problem.

Your tantrum yesterday concerning the milk was totally justified, and my nose deserved to be broken by the microwave oven you hurled at me. You never would have made the error I did because compared to me, as you've pointed out innumerable times, you are perfect.

The milk blunder was totally unworthy of me, forgetfulness being only one of my many faults you've justifiably specified, in addition to me having low self-esteem, being sloppy, and not being sufficiently concerned about your flatulence.

I humbly bow down to you, an act you've insisted on for me to honor your regal presence as a princess, which you've been deservedly treated as since you were a little girl.

I am passionate for you, me being one of the many men who have demonstrated passion for you, even the multitude that spent just one night with you.

The result: complete forgiveness. "You're so understanding," she allowed Barnaby.

Plus Mrs. Zill made his favorite desserts for the next week, including the cakes they both washed down with 2% reduced fat milk.

Now I've mentioned earlier that this book does not deal with arguments, but only reaction to *minor* offences. But, for illustrative purposes, here's an example of what a reasonable husband (*again Barnaby Zill*) once delivered to his wife after a *major* argument:

I was totally amiss in having that affair with Bambi, my graduate assistant. If I was a truly honest person I'd have realized that it was childish for me to try and get back at you for the multiple liaisons you've enjoyed over the years with others. You are much prettier than Bambi, though not as pretty as Nancy, Shelby, Becky, Marilyn (there were two of them – Marilyn B and Marilyn L), Carol, Joannie, Kaila, and I suppose about ten others I can't recall whose names began with A to M, and another ten with N to Z.

I remember the first time I ever kissed you. It was on our third anniversary. Though I wish you would have let me kiss your lips instead of your toes.

Men don't have affairs just because of sex. They do it for other reasons, like to feel important, and I feel so important on the two times a year you consent to mattress with me – New Year's Eve, when you get drunk on champagne, and July 4, when you get drunk on beer. But I understand that you do have other friends you need to treat well.

I loved the pretend games we played at those times – you pretending you were a sack of potatoes. You were so real. I get swallowed up in our love-making. There is so much of you to feel passionate about. All 300 pounds of you.

Unfortunately, Barnaby did not obtain complete forgiveness. "That was not heartfelt," she complained. "It was much too passive-aggressive." (*While Barnaby was busy getting his degree in arithmetic, she took some psychology classes.*)

In fact, he obtained no forgiveness at all. Nor did he obtain any desserts except Jello and sherbet, the soft foods he was allowed to eat after Mrs. Zill busted his jaw.

I suppose this behavior on her part illustrates one of two things, or both:

- Women are not always consistent in providing forgiveness
- Apology, even an elaborate one, may not work as well after the more serious argument.

One further approach. If you set up the situation correctly, it may not be necessary to put together different word combinations or a long story. Wrong, sorry, love may suffice.

CAN 'I'M WRONG. I'M SORRY. I LOVE YOU' BE USED AS A CODE?

You know how couples often repeat sweet things to each other, or have endearing routines (*not just nicknames*) that express coupleness – something between them with special meanings that they share, that bring them together.

I know one couple where every night, just before turning into bed, Josh says to his wife Candy, "You're the best wife in the whole wide world."

And Candy, in return, says to Josh, "You're the best husband in the whole wide world." (*Of course, just to mix things up, alternately she compliments him first.*)

Then Josh and Candy turn into bed followed by whatever type of turning they feel like doing that night.

What *isn't* important is that they be accurate. I mean how can one prove that one's mate is the best wife or husband in the world? Do they know all the husbands and wives in the world so they have a strong basis of comparison? And what are the criteria? And are the criteria different in different countries of the whole wide world?

Is what makes a great spouse within the United States the same as what makes a great spouse in Scotland? Someone who has the skill of cleaning out their spouse's bagpipe in Scotland wouldn't be as prized in the United States (*where spouses clean out their spouse's saxophone*), or Israel (*where cleaning out a shofar is prized*), or Venezuela (*I don't know what they clean out there except capitalists*), or Mazinstan. (*OK, I made up Mazinstan because I have a friend named Stan Mazin, who is such a great guy that he deserves to have a country named after him.*)

Getting back to Josh and Candy -- what *is* important was that each of them understood that the words they spoke exemplified they had this connection where each cared for and respected the other. The words brought them closer together, and if there was any tension between them, it didn't matter anymore.

So, maybe you can somehow accomplish your spouse never getting tired of you saying, "I'm wrong. I'm sorry. I love you."

You and your mate can mutually agree that, "I'm wrong. I'm sorry. I love you" is a *code*, a *shorthand understanding* symbolizing a joint desire to dissipate or smooth out or otherwise eliminate your conflict and resume lovey-dovey.

Perhaps another way of putting this is that you two agree to disagree about the subject that has rifted you because your relationship is more important than any reason that caused a squabble. And now that rift has gone pffffft.

That is, when you're saying the magical phrase, you *both* understand that the third element *('I love you')* the most important element, applies, and, "Let's get over this stupid rift that's keeping us from happiness and mattressing."

In this sense, saying "I'm wrong. I'm sorry. I love you" is code for what you truly mean, which is, "I'm wrong. I'm sorry. I love you."

That makes sense, doesn't it?

ARE WOMEN REALLY THAT DIFFERENT FROM MEN?

I'll now make a single blanket statement, a profound one, the summary result of behavioral scrutinizations I've made over my lifetime, helped along by my years of psychology education and study of consumer behavior. No, no, don't call me brilliant for this observation. Others might have discovered this just as easily had they lived my life. Here it is:

WOMEN REALLY ARE DIFFERENT FROM MEN!

Please, please don't even begin to argue. Even ardent feminists, affirmative action adherents, MSNBC analysts, and the most progressive of political pundits would have to agree with my observation.

Sometimes the 'different' is just that – not the same. And sometimes the 'different' has an added dimension – that one gender is superior to the other in some way.

I've compiled such a list (*no doubt not exhaustive*) of ways women are different from men. Of course, each item listed is not true for *all* women or *all* men. But generalizations about women as a group that generally hold up include:

Attractive women are termed 'pretty' or 'beautiful', while attractive men are 'handsome'. (So if a woman is called 'handsome' it means she looks at least somewhat like a man.)

Women are less strong than men. (Though Barnaby Zill's wife can bench press him)

Women can't jump as high as men. (Except when they spy a spider or mouse)

Women can't run as fast as men. (Except when chased by a monster in a horror movie)

Women can't grow a thick mustache. (Most women can do a very wispy one, but not bushy)

Women have larger breasts than most men. (Yes, <u>most</u> men)

Women pee differently than men (which is why the bathroom for Women at a restaurant doesn't have a urinal. How do I know that? Because I once accidentally entered such a bathroom. That was the time I received a concussion from the attack of a half-dressed crazy feminist. Which didn't make sense – aren't feminists supposed to be about equality?)

Women are more capable of giving birth than most men (Duh! To state the obvious).

Women have a lower pain threshold than men (with the exception of childbirth, where women can tolerate a pain level that would cause men to faint.)

Women are more competitive about their clothes than men. (Here's my evidence: If two women discover they're wearing the exact same dress design and color at an affair they will resent each other. But two men wearing the exact same design and color suit *could care less about the other man's clothes.)*

Women (well, girls) are much more likely to play with dolls, while it's wimpy for a true man (well, boy) to play with dolls. (Males play with action figures, for goodness sakes, not dolls.)

Women are much more likely to apply perfume to entice the opposite gender. (True men would never use perfume, for goodness sakes. They apply cologne.)

Women are much better at multitasking. (For example, my wife Rebecca can do the laundry, prepare to bake a cake from scratch, and have a lengthy telephone conversation, <u>all at the same time</u>. I could manage just one of these without screwing up bad trying another.)

Women's brain wiring is different from that of men. While their brain size is smaller, there are more connections. (Neurologists have demonstrated the existence of these differences in brain construction. These differences explain why women are better at multitasking, but not as good at math, which requires focus. Barnaby Zill's wife couldn't count calories, which is maybe partially how she got to the point she could bench press Barnaby.)

Women talk more than men. (Formal research studies indicate it's about three times as much. But even stronger evidence is that when I talk on the phone with my friends the conversation lasts maybe five minutes, while when Rebecca is on the phone with her friends it lasts a half hour. She even talks fifteen minutes with <u>my</u> friends.)

Women listen more than men. (Maybe because they like to talk, and in order to be fair to the person they are talking to they have to listen every once in a while.)

Women communicate better than men. (Of course they do. They have all this practice talking.)

Women express emotion more than men, and not only crying. (Partially because they like to talk more, as just indicated. Also, because until recent years it wasn't macho manly for a man to express any sad emotions.)

Women have more friends than men, especially male friends, if they are promiscuous. (Another reason women talk more than men.)

Women confide in friends more, this going beyond the fact they have more friends. (But partially due to their liking to talk more often.)

Women are more empathetic than men. (Gives them another opportunity to talk, and material to gossip.)

Women gossip more than men. (Read the above.)

Women are less likely to take chances, and more concerned about self-preservation. (Which is maybe why most lottery winners are men, while women are more likely than men to shop at the grocery.)

Women like to resolve situations, while men are more likely to think sticky situations will no doubt pass and resolve themselves if you don't talk about them. (Another reason why women talk more than men.)

Women are the caretakers of the home, more responsible for a happy emotional environment (while the men are out hunting and gathering).

Women like to research, accumulating gads of information, more than men do. They are more curious, more risk averse and concerned about making the wrong decision. (In shopping, for example, women are more likely than men to search the Internet for info about products and prices. Surprising, eh? Thought nerds were mostly men?)

Women are more apt to like to shop than men. They visit more different stores than men and enjoy the shopping process. Men merely go to a store that carries the product they want to buy and, bam, just buy it! (Go to any department store or supermarket. Is there ever a majority of men?)

Women are more complex than men, harder to decipher. (Isn't a husband much more likely to say, "I can't figure her out" than a wife to say, "I can't figure him out"?)

So, where does this all lead regarding male vs. female usage of "Wrong, sorry, love."?

Remember, it's clear that for a variety of reasons women talk more than men. They also don't want to take the risk of the same situation arising again, causing tension around the home. Due to brain wiring and experience, they are more complex than men, wanting to further explore a given situation. And so, when a man gives the "Wrong, sorry, love" speech to a woman she may want to talk further about it. As mentioned earlier in this manual, she may even have the nerve to tell the male apologist something like, "It's wonderful for you to say that. But what are we going to do to prevent this type of dumbass behavior of yours from happening again"?

As I said, she *may* say something like this. Just in case she does, now the male has to undertake conversation, a territory women are much more comfortable existing in and gifted with. He must be prepared to have this discussion, and be grilled in detail about every word he uses, every thought he promulgates.

Ugh!

On the other hand, if the woman initiates the "Wrong, sorry, love" stuff, the man's reaction most likely will be to think, "I've won. Woo-hoo!" (*Although he thinks it, he won't say it aloud in the moment, since that would likely result in something being tossed at his head, even if it's just words of rebuke and accusation from his mate, who doesn't want to be perceived as a loser. So, the best response for the man is to say something like, "I accept your apology. Let's mattress!"*)

Putting this all together, from the man's perspective saying "Wrong, sorry, love" means you might be taking your chances, and you might be better off just clamming up. But if you totally clam up your squabble won't be resolved. So, you've gotta take that chance, and hope you won't be pulled into a serious discussion.

From your mate's perspective, your saying "Wrong, sorry, love" means she'll be entering a discussion she's probably much better prepared for than you. That's good for her. But what might be even better for you is when she's the one instituting "Wrong, sorry, love," since it may very well result in you saying, "Let's mattress!"

IS USING 'I'M WRONG. I'M SORRY. I LOVE YOU' MANIPULATIVE?

Of course it is!

In a sense.

OK. Totally!

What is 'manipulating' people, anyway? It's action you take which gets someone else to think or act in a manner you'd like them to. People manipulate others all the time, even if it's subconsciously.

Barnaby Zill invariably tells his wife she's great cook when he takes a rare meal break from his busy work as an arithmetician. Because of this reinforcement she continues making luscious dishes. Never gets tired of cooking for him (*unless they have a squabble, or worse, an argument*).

Is that 'manipulation'?

Absolutely! At least according to the definition I've provided.

But is it bad? Unethical? Unfair?

I think not. Mrs. Zill doesn't think so either.

Manipulation is only a negative act when it causes a person to think or act in a certain way ruinous to their well-being. So, if 'wrong, sorry, love' enhances or heals a relationship, or resolves a glitch in a prior strong bond between two lovely people, should it be considered toxic?

Not at all!

Still, there's a negative connotation to the word 'manipulation' and its family sister words of the same root – manipulate, manipulative, manipulator, manipulatable, manipulatization, manipulatism, manipulatification, etc.. (*No, as Barnaby Zill would point out, 'multiplication' is not a member of that family.*)

Perhaps a more acceptable way of considering the 'Wrong, sorry, love' approach is that it's not manipulative, but a way of 'handling people,', or 'management skill.'

The problem comes when your mate *thinks* you are being manipulative. That you're using trickery of some sort to get her to behave in a certain way harmful to her. People like to think that they have their own minds and aren't subject to the machinations of others. Maybe that it's OK for them to be manipulative, but not to be the victim of others' efforts.

So, after you've manipulated her, don't let her know what you've just managed to do. Don't brag about it -- "Ha-ha! I've just manipulated you into…".

You can't help it if she figures it out on her own. But don't help her along.

If she does think you are trying to manipulate her *("I'm not stupid! You think you're so clever, trying to manipulate me. But I see right through you.")* just deny it. Strongly. Act surprised, even offended, that she'd even think of you trying to do that! Show disappointment that she'd accuse you, that she'd infer toxic motivations to you which don't exist. If you're good at bringing forth moisture in your eyes, add that.

ion, "I'm wrong, I'm sorry. I love you."

In response, tell her you accept her apology, thank her for it, add that it was quite mature for her to do so, and if the two of you are in mutual mood, head for the mattress.

Hold on a second. Reconsidering – don't tell her it was mature of her, for that will give her the opening to accuse you of accusing her of being immature in the past, thereby causing another tiff to squabble.

Just head for the mattress.

WILL THIS MANUAL MAKE THE WORLD A BETTER PLACE?

Really, will this manual make the world a better place?

Maybe.

Remember the butterfly in Africa who flapped his wings, causing a grain of dirt to rise, and the upshot of all that, once one thing led to another many times, was that a farmer, Bertram Zill in Kansas, belched just before he was swallowed by a tornado? (*By extraordinary coincidence, Bertram Zill just happened to be Barnaby's uncle.*)

Or, suppose Barnaby Zill was making mattress with his wife, and the two of them were startled by a loud thunderclap, the storm an ultimate result of that butterfly's flapping. This disturbance occurred just before the baby they were about to create was conceived, and thus little Juniper, who was to be a genius, was never born, and the cure for cancer was never discovered until years later? And born instead, because a different sperm reached the egg, was gigolo Marcus Zill, who couldn't even add single digit numbers accurately, causing his father to fall on the sword while in the midst of eating sushi. (*If you're going to fall on the sword – a Japanese custom that you follow if you're totally ashamed – why not do it when eating Japanese food?*)

So, you never know how one behavior will affect the world later on. I mean if a single butterfly's momentary action could cause all that, what can the more elaborate action of a human being do?

Let's examine what might happen to the world now that this manual is published.

We can start by listing some major subjects relevant to what's going on in the world today. All issues that need to be addressed.

>   Peace on earth
>   World financial stability
>   Bee crisis
>   World hunger
>   Literacy

Climate change
Religious extremism
Disaster prediction
Population control

I won't address them directly in this manual. But let's examine what *might* happen as a result of its readership. Not *will*, but *might*.

Peace On Earth
This manual preaches peace. Its intention is to restore peace after a squabble has taken place.

Now, a single relationship is just one instance of engendering peace. But now add in an enormous number of relationships that now have become peaceful, once this manual is translated into multiple languages and sales multiply exponentially. Now we've gotten somewhere.

Peace will be on people's minds. It will become a social media sensation. Go viral!

And there may be a tipping point where enough peaceful relationships occur that momentum results in the world becoming a much more peaceful place. It's more than the norm. It's expected.

Now, if we can only get this manual into the hands of some of those dictators in foreign countries! Or the heads of US Congressional committees.

And, hey, maybe we can get one of those Miss America contestants to be the spokesperson for the world peace movement.

Financial stability
Because of this manual, and its emphasis on love and togetherness, money will become less important all around the world.

Oh, it will still be important to some, like the Koch brothers and the Buffett family, but overall happy and productive people will become less interested in accumulating money, and so financial crises will be eliminated in most countries except on some islands in Micronesia where the currency is shells anyway.

Bee crisis and world hunger

It is becoming apparent that the number of bees is diminishing, and with fewer of them around, not as many plants are being fertilized. There is less edible food being grown.

An engineer for an oil company will read this manual, resulting in some wonderful all-night mattressing with his wife to the point where he oversleeps the next morning. Because he's still in bed, workers at his company's fracking operation will overfrack, causing a substantial earthquake. This will result in a wall falling somewhere and almost crushing a bee. But the bee won't be killed.

Instead, slight changes will be made to its DNA so that when that bee and its descendants reproduce they'll be resistant to the pesticides that have been diminishing the bee population. The DNA modification will also magnify the bees' sex drive so their reproductive rate will grow enormously. Bees will now flourish. The bee population will reverse its prior numerical decline, and fertilization of plants all over the world will increase dramatically, eliminating world hunger.

Literacy

Many people around the world are illiterate. This includes folks in many Western countries. (*Obviously this does not include you, unless maybe you are being read to.*)

So, after this book is published, and word gets around about how it improves relationships, men who are now illiterate will be motivated to learn to read and obtain its magical secrets.

This will happen all over the world.

Men will have time to be educated since they won't have to spend so much time worrying about their next meal, due to the plethora of food engendered by the now huge bee population.

Of course, more people will suffer stings, but that's a small price to pay for so many not going hungry, and being able to read, and for the price of honey to decline so more people can afford it.

Other Issues

Meanwhile, now that Barnaby is gone, Mrs. Zill will fool with Barnaby's advisor, and when the earthquake hits, they'll go back and forth on the mattress, ultimately conceiving quadruplets – Horace, Boris, Morris, and Doris.

Horace will be a world-class expert in reversing climate change.

Boris will devise systems to accurately predict when earthquakes will occur and how strong. Later, he'll be able to predict the same for hurricanes, and in memory of his granduncle-in-law Bertram, tornadoes.

Morris will become an expert in converting religious extremists into antique store proprietors and accountants.

Doris, the sister, will be an expert in population control, though she may not be as successful as her siblings in mitigating the issue she's expert in. She'll have a tough time resolving that problem of overpopulation.

Population Control

You may be aware that the more people populate our planet Earth the greater the depletion of natural resources. Doris will know about that.

Not just oil or other fossil fuels. But less clean water available to shampoo hair. Shortages of asparagus and limes.

Sad to say, but I've got to admit it. As Doris will point out, this book is deleterious to population control. Why is that? Because this manual is designed to bring couples closer together. The more couples get along with each other, and resolve squabbles, the more likely they are to be making mattress, which then results in making babies.

So be careful if you don't want any little critters at the moment.

To mitigate this population increase, to make it less likely, I considered inserting condoms into pockets in the back inside cover of this manual. But my editor sent the following note: "Placing condoms in the book might present liability exposure should the rubbers leak or break. I speak from personal experience with leakage or breakage. My mom said I was a rubber defect accident. They never wanted me. I've felt inferior my whole life, after she told me that. Why did you even bring it up? Do you want to ruin my life more than my mom already did?"

So I dropped the condom idea.

At any rate, now that you have this manual it might be a good idea to drop in on your local drugstore.

Now, let's examine people less intelligent and educated than you, the reader. They are not reading this manual and therefore their couple confrontations are lasting longer than you smarter folks. This means less opportunity for mattressing and fewer amounts of babies.

Isn't that strange, more educated people having more babies than less educated people!

What? Less educated people have more babies?

Well, not quite.

Since they are not so smart to begin with they're less likely to use birth control, resulting in more babies. But this just evens out those dumbbells who have less mattressing, and thus, fewer babies. It's a wash.

In other words, as Doris will point out, "No conclusive proof exits that buying Shulman's book has any net effect on world population growth among stupid people, but there is evidence that it has a harmful effect on population control among the intelligencia."

Now you may think all of the above is ridiculous, that none of the issues raised will be influenced by this book, that this manual will really make the world a better or worse place overall (*except for the men heeding its advice*). Realistically, none of what I've described can possibly happen, you may think.

But how realistic was it that that butterfly in Africa subsequently caused Bertram Zill in Kansas to belch just before he was swallowed by a tornado?

WILL THERE BE A SEQUEL TO THIS MANUAL?

It would be titled:

I'M WRONG.

I'M SORRY.

I LOVE YOU.

How to get along with your mate after a squabble.

A survival manual for **WOMEN.**

Not a chance!

Most women would never buy such a book.

Why?

Women never *(OK, hardly ever)* admit they're wrong.

At least way less often than men. (*Not that most men really think they're wrong.*)

Instead, women will try to turn your presentations of fact into a 'matter of opinion.'

Even when confronted with undeniable, irrefutable, indisputable evidence they won't say, "I'm wrong."

They might say "You're right", but not "I'm wrong."

Absent of undeniable, irrefutable, indisputable evidence, forget about it altogether. Even one of them saying, "You're right."

They like to hear it, but not say it.

Not sure if it's genetic.

HOW SHOULD YOU DEAL WITH YOUR RESERVATIONS?

It's clear that many men will have reservations about telling their mate, "I'm wrong. I'm sorry. I love you."

If that's the case with you, if any of these reservations is preventing you from gaining the benefits of the advice presented thus far, well then, let's discuss some of these reservations.

You don't want to be with her anymore
Sometimes relationships must come to an end.

Alas, alas, alas.

For whatever reason, you don't want to be with your mate any longer. Maybe she's too messy, too picky, unfaithful, not interested in football, spends too much money, unreliable, ambitionless, argumentative, wears only turquoise.

Or maybe you are like that, and you can't stand that she tells you in no uncertain terms what you are like.

Whatever, you've decided after serious thought (*and not just because of this recent little squabble*) that you desire your relationship to end.

This manual was created to bring a couple back together after a rift. But if you really don't want to get back together, **don't say**, "I'm wrong. I'm sorry. I love you."

Let the relationship end.

But let's go on to the more likely scenarios – situations where you want to be with her harmoniously, and this squabble has temporarily gotten in the way.

After all, that's why you bought this manual, isn't it?

I don't think I'm wrong in this instance
So what if you're not wrong in this instance!

Which is more important to you, being right on this minor issue, or having a satisfying relationship with your mate? A relationship which usually keeps you both happy.

Use your brain, kiddo!

The brain that's in your head. And to your good fortune, this may lead to using the brain that women often jokingly say you have between your legs.

I don't think I'm ever wrong
If you think you are never wrong, you're wrong about that. Which proves you are not never wrong.

Everyone is wrong about something sometimes.

You are a human being, so you make mistakes.

So, you are lying to yourself with this attitude, aren't you?

I don't want to admit I'm wrong
By this attitude you're admitting you're vain. You're willing to sacrifice the happiness you'd have with your mate just so you won't have to admit you were wrong!

Don't you know that no one, including your mate, will think less of you if you admit you are wrong every once in a while.

Don't be a nitwit. You don't have one as a mate. So, why should you be one?

I don't want to discuss with her the event causing the rift
It's probably true that she's more skillful at discussion than you are. As I pointed out earlier, women have a lot more experience talking than men do.

This does not mean that you have to give in to whatever she wants. You can think logically, can't you? So, use that logical mind of yours to get to where you want to go, what you want to happen.

I don't like to follow someone else's advice
What? You are the most brilliant person in the world, knowledgeable about how one should behave in every instance?

Admit it! You sometimes don't know what's best for you. And if you refuse to take good advice because you think it's an admission that someone is smarter than you, then you're not so smart, are you?

I think my mate will think of me as wimpy
She won't think of you as wimpy!

She'll admire you.

She'll be so thankful that you have sufficient self-esteem to admit you are wrong and to apologize. Sometimes it takes a real man to deal with a situation straight on.

I will think of myself as wimpy, not a 'real man'
See the above.

If she won't think of you as a wimp, why should you think of yourself that way?

I don't want to be manipulative
Manipulating people refers to actions you take which get someone else to think or act in a manner you'd like them to.

You praise certain behaviors of others to get them to repeat the positive behavior. Isn't reinforcement manipulation?

You ask questions which leads someone to behave in a beneficial way.

I discussed this before, pointing out that, yes, the magical 'I'm wrong, etc.' is manipulative, but so what! People manipulate others all the time, even if it's subconsciously.

But is it bad? Unethical? Unfair?

Manipulation is only a negative act when causing a person to think or act in a certain way is deleterious to their well-being. So, if 'wrong, sorry, love' enhances or heals a relationship, resolves a glitch in a previously strong bond between two lovely people, should it be considered deleterious?

Not at all!

So, don't worry about being manipulative.

Besides, she has no qualms about manipulating you, does she?

I don't like to think some writer knows more than me
Do you think you know more about any and all subjects than every other person? Than people who have devoted much thought to a given subject.

OK, sometimes you do. But most of the time you defer to experts.

And you should in this instance. Don't let your jealousy of me, just because I'm married to Rebecca and you aren't, serve to diminish your happiness.

After all, just because I'm married to a woman who is beautiful, smart, creative, empathetic, encouraging, and reliable, shouldn't affect your relationship. You and I are two separate people.

And, anyway, isn't your mate just like Rebecca in many of these ways?

OK, no!

But I bet she is in some of these ways.

Be thankful.

It simply won't work
How will you know it doesn't work unless you try it?

How sure are you that you'll be wasting your time implementing this manual's suggestions?

After all, you've gotten this far in the book. Don't you think you should give it a try?

So, arrange to squabble with your mate (*but not to the extent that it's an argument*) and see what happens.

No, that's stupid! Don't arrange to squabble. Just try out my advice the next time you have one.

I know procrastination will work
It's true. Sometimes procrastination, delaying making or implementing that decision, works. But sometimes it doesn't, even makes things worse.

Here's how it *may not* work:

Procrastination results in the unresolved rift festering, growing more rotten each hour, negative thoughts piled on, morphing, mutating, into a hideous situation that's much more difficult to manage than the original squabble.

In that case, assuming you really want to restore your relationship, procrastination is a poor idea. You should've dealt with the rift situation before it became uglier.

Now, here's how procrastination *may* work:

You decide to wait her out. She does the same to you. Time passes, and you both forget the rift altogether.

Maybe this is how your relationship has evolved up until now. Letting yourselves cool down, and realizing that whatever caused you two to squabble isn't at all as important as being together with each other.

The squabble dissipates.

In that event, maybe you don't need this manual.

Too bad it took you this long to find that out.

But the good thing is that your relationship is still intact, healthy, and even flourishing. Which is my goal in preparing this manual, to bring couples together.

So, I've succeeded.

I'm so brilliant!

DO I TAKE MY OWN ADVICE ABOUT WRONG, SORRY, LOVE?

Of course not!

To behave according to the expression, "I'm wrong. I'm sorry. I love you" I'd have to admit I was wrong right away. But my own wife, the **beautiful, talented, insightful, remarkable Rebecca,** thinks *that I think* I'm never wrong.

She's wrong about that (*so she's not always insightful*). But the point is she thinks it's true. So, if I approached her with an admission that I was wrong, she'd first feel my forehead to take my temperature. But then finding normal heat she'd become highly suspicious, assuming there was something up she needed to be extremely watchful about.

Later, she might search my pockets for motel receipts, my smart phone for incriminating text messages, the glove compartment of my car for panties, credit card charges for purchases from adult bookstores, and who knows what else? This going beyond what I was referring to when I told her I was wrong.

I don't want that level of scrutiny.

Not that she'd find anything.

Probably.

Ha-ha, not really.

There are two expressions that steer my life, keep me on the right path. One is, "A doctor who treats himself has a fool for a patient."

See the connection? What I prescribe for others is not necessarily the best treatment for me. So, this book is really for others.

The second expression is, "Do as I say, not as I do." So, it follows that I expect you, the reader, to follow my advice, if you can make any sense of it. But you should ignore what I actually do in practice.

So, no, I don't listen to myself, and don't follow the content of this book. (*Hear that, Rebecca?*)

But you, the reader, should.

GET THAT REBECCA? YOU DON'T HAVE TO WORRY ABOUT ME USING MY TECHNIQUES WITH YOU. YOU WOULD SEE RIGHT THROUGH ME. YOU'RE MUCH TOO SMART TO FALL FOR ANY FORM OF MANIPULATION.

SO, YOU DON'T HAVE TO READ ANY FURTHER. STOP HERE. IT'LL BE A WASTE OF YOUR TIME TO CONTINUE.

JUST CLOSE THE BOOK, AND GO ON TO SOMETHING ELSE.

THE NEXT CHAPTER IS BORING, ANYWAY.

YOU ARE A BUSY WOMAN, WITH LOTS OF PROJECTS TO KEEP YOU BUSY.

SO, GO OFF, THEN. DO WHAT YOU WERE MEANT TO DO. CREATE SOMETHING WONDERFUL.

NO, I DON'T MEAN COOK ME DINNER, OR WASH MY SOCKS.

HA-HA. YOU ARE MUCH MORE CAPABLE OF ARTISTRY THAN THAT.

GO DO YOUR THING!

THE REAL TRUTH

OK, is she gone?

Now I can tell the truth.

My stepdaughter says I should be my best customer and talk about my successes in handling my wife.

So, here's the skinny.

The truth is, what I said on the prior pages is the truth.

I can't use my advice with her.

She's much more insightful than me. If she wrote a book on the same subject she'd give much better advice than I ever could.

She's a joy! She's a whiz!

I just hope she doesn't come out with her book before this manual is published.

OK, REBECCA, YOU CAN LEAVE NOW. I KNOW MY EARLIER SUGGESTION THAT YOU STOP READING AROUSED YOUR SUSPICION.

YOU GOT ME!

I'M WRONG. I'M SORRY. I LOVE YOU!

HA-HA.

SEEYA LATER.

I ROTATED THE MATTRESS.

www.ingramcontent.com/pod-product-compliance
Lightning Source LLC
Chambersburg PA
CBHW041430300426
44114CB00007B/96